USAIN BOLT

USAIN BOLT

LEGEND

First published in Jamaica 2017 by
Ian Randle Publishers
16 Herb McKenley Drive
Box 686
Kingston 6
www.ianrandlepublishers.com

© 2017 The Gleaner Company (Media) Limited
ISBN: 978-976-637-951-3 (hbk)
       978-976-637-953-7 (pbk)

National Library of Jamaica Cataloguing-In-Publication Data
The Gleaner Company (Media) Limited.
    Usain Bolt : legend / The Gleaner Company (Media) Limited.

       p. : ill. ; cm
ISBN 978-976-637-951-3

1. Bolt, Usain, 1986-
2. Bolt, Usain, 1986- – Pictorial works
3. Runners (Sports) – Jamaica – Biography
4. Sprinting – Jamaica
I. Title

796.422092   - dc 23

Publication of this book has been made possible by a generous contribution
from the Culture, Health, Arts, Sports and Education Fund, Jamaica.

Photographs © The Gleaner Company (Media) Limited, Associated Press,
Leroy Gray and Racers Track Club except where otherwise noted.

Cover and Book Design by Ian Randle Publishers
Re-printed in Great Britain, 2017

The Gleaner
Company (Media) Limited

Dedicated to
Usain St Leo Bolt,
a true Legend,
by *The Gleaner Company
(Media) Limited*
on behalf of a proud
and grateful nation.

CONTENTS

FASTEST MAN ALIVE

U sain Bolt is world famous for his multiple victories on and off the track. Naturally, the fastest man in history over the 100m and 200m sprints, he has earned numerous accolades locally, regionally and internationally. In February 2017, he was named the Laureus Sportsman of the Year for the fourth time.

While that global honour has doubtless made Bolt feel richly rewarded, *The Gleaner* is also proud to claim a hand in another triple for the fastest man the world has ever seen. Also in February 2017, he was again named the 2016 'Man of the Year' by the oldest newspaper in the English-speaking Caribbean, as he was for 2008 and 2009. We are happy to note that communications giant Radio Jamaica, our partner in the *RJRGleaner Communications Group*, also named Bolt 'Sportsman of the Year' for 2016, adding to his wins for 2008, 2009, 2011, 2012, 2013 and 2015.

I am pleased to have guided *The Gleaner* as Editor-in-Chief throughout this period when Bolt has astounded all with his athletic prowess, threatening to exhaust our headline writers' creative use of his name to memorably sum up one superb performance after the other. The maxim that journalism is the first rough draft of history holds true, but we have gone a step further to cull Usain Bolt's athletic history from our reams of newsprint (on him) to present a refined, polished, compact yet comprehensive history of the greatest sprinter of all time.

The publication also validates the continued importance of print media, its transportability and transferability from one reader to another, making it irreplaceable.

It is not a reclaiming of Usain Bolt as a Jamaican, for while conquering all-comers on the track worldwide, he has always made it clear that he is from the 'land of wood and water', the black, green and gold flag draped over his broad shoulders. And where else could this unforgettable victory pose, lithe limbs extended and engaging personality enthralling global audiences come from other than an irrepressible Jamaican spirit?

This book was conceptualised as a statement that Usain Bolt has an athletic history at 'yard' before the world stage, and rich, deep Jamaican roots that have sustained him throughout an unprecedented period of global sprinting dominance. He is one of the countless Jamaican athletes whose performances have been reported on for decades in this newspaper, from smaller development meets to the competitive cauldron of the annual Boys and Girls' Athletic Championships, then regional meets like the CARIFTA Games and global contests. *The Gleaner* is part of the foundation of that rich Jamaican athletics tradition which Bolt epitomises.

I am satisfied that *The Gleaner* is part of a Jamaican-based training and support services system – a happy departure from former times – which has resulted in the global athletics supremacy of which Usain Bolt is a part. He lives and trains at home and this defining story is being told from home by Jamaicans.

As Usain Bolt's career winds down on his terms, I consider this book part of a relay, a figurative handing off by the perennial 4x100m anchor man to his country as a whole, and the next generation of Jamaican athletes in particular. For excellence has to be learned and patterned for effective succession. *The Gleaner* has done what no one else has – keeping up with Bolt from his student days at William Knibb Memorial High School to meets in far-flung places of the world, and you hold that trajectory in your hands.

We have had lots of pleasure along the way and trust that you will, too.

Garfield Grandison
Editor-in-Chief, *The Gleaner*
April 2017

THOSE WHO HELPED

Capturing rich history and precious moments in 208 pages is never an easy feat – especially when sprint sensation Usain Bolt is the subject.

However, once again, *The Gleaner,* with the contribution of so many, has risen to the occasion to produce a fine publication on an outstanding world-famous athlete.

It all started three years ago when Ricardo Makyn, Multimedia Photo Editor at *The Gleaner,* approached Editor-in-Chief Garfield Grandison about the need for *The Gleaner* – the oldest media house in the Western Hemisphere – to do 'something' to honour Bolt on his official retirement from track and field.

It was his insistence that led to *Usain Bolt: Legend.*

There are several astute persons, filled with verve and vigour, who contributed to this project. First and foremost, project leader Garfield Grandison, who was supported by publisher Ian Randle, did a sterling job of managing this project and ensuring it was completed within deadline.

We recognise the efforts of photo coordinator Ricardo Makyn, supported by information system manager Sheree Rhoden and her assistant Ahon Gray for compiling the best photos of Bolt redolent of his superb performances.

We salute the work of Susan Daley for coordinating the research on Bolt and his many journeys. We also laud the outstanding work done by the writers, assistant sport editor Elton Tucker and sport editor Andre Lowe; Robert Lalah, special content editor; Hubert Lawrence, sports broadcaster and writer; Ian Boyne, columnist and public affairs commentator; Martin Henry, columnist and university administrator, Arnold Bertram, historian and author; and proofreaders Ronald Berry and Andre Wright.

We thank cartoonist Las May for his contribution of the whimsical cartoons he sketched to add to the diversity of this book.

This project could not have been completed without the contribution of the CHASE Fund and other gracious sponsors. We thank them for believing and investing in not only this project but our culture and sports.

We make special mention of Shernett Robinson, special projects editor and sponsorship coordinator, for interfacing with sponsors from the outset of this project.

The Gleaner extends special gratitude to Usain and his Management team for their endorsement of this undertaking. It certainly meant a lot to us, and served as a motivator for the entire team.

USAIN BOLT, LEGEND

Blazing out of Sherwood Content, southern Trelawny, Jamaica, powered, some say, by yellow yam, Dr the Honourable Usain St Leo Bolt, OJ,CD LLD (Hon), has taken speed to the world.

Olympic 'triple triple' sprint gold: 100m, 200m, 4x100m relay. Beijing 2008, London 2012, Rio 2016, and in a hundred other meets, there has never been another sprint talent like Bolt. The first and only athlete to smash three Olympic and world records at the Games. Speed performance not seen since the restoration of the Olympic Games in 1896 in Athens, Greece, the country where the Games began in the 8th century BC.

Bolt, world record holder for the 100m, 9.58. Running just one short of 50 sub-10-second races in his scintillating career. Only two others having more sub-10s, one his countryman, Asafa Powell.

Bolt, world record holder for the 200m, 19.19. The only man in Olympic history to win the 200m more than once, Beijing 2008 and London 2012. Then Rio 2016 for the third time. Legend.

The world may have to wait another hundred years for his equal. Will we ever see his better? Perhaps only after human speed performance is bioengineered!

Bolt, trademark flash of lightning copied around the world. Fun-loving showman, delighting the world on and off the track.

Bolt, inherited family name, uncannily fit for purpose. Lightning Bolt. But who would have known? Not his parents who middle-named him 'St Leo'. Man who would race with the heart of a lion. With the speed, stamina, focus and the courage of a thoroughbred.

'Usain', 'beautiful', from its possible Arabic origins. Unusual name – but not surprising –

for a Jamaican child born among a people pulled from everywhere, blended together here, borrowing from everywhere, and taking it to the world. Powerful, lean and mean frame, 6 ft 5", rippling muscles, face study in super-concentration, unmatched human speed. A beautiful choreography of human physical and mental performance, blazing down the track – in front.

From sleepy Sherwood Content in deep rural Jamaica, Cockpit Country, to the world. Born August 21, 1986. Waldensia Primary School, running in the annual national primary schools track meet. By 12 and graduation, Waldensia's fastest runner for the 100m.

On to William Knibb Memorial High School, named after the great Emancipator, William Knibb, OM. Knibb was awarded the Order of Merit in 1988, the 150th anniversary of 'Full Free' for his anti-slavery work in Bolt's parish. Usain Bolt, Order of Distinction, Commander Class, 2008; Order of Jamaica and Ambassador-at-Large, 2009, at 23. Doctor of Letters *Honoris Causa*: stellar performance in athletics.

Bolt, the greatest of the Jamaican athletes since our debut at the Olympics, London, 1948. Wint, gold, 400m. McKenley, silver, 400m. Wint, silver, 800m. Since '48, 78 Olympic medals. Bolt, eight. All gold. Bolt, the undisputed king of the 'Sprint Factory of the World'. Little island in the sun, only 2.7 million strong. Bolt, the greatest athlete of all time.

Wint, McKenley, streets named in their honour around the National Stadium where Usain Bolt first sprinted to national attention, aged 15, Inter-Secondary Schools Boys and Girls Championships, 2001, 200m silver, 22.02 seconds. To the world, World Junior Championships, 2002, Kingston, Jamaica, 200m gold. At 15, the youngest World Junior gold medallist ever.

Sculptor Alvin Marriott's *'Athlete'*, rising to his stride in front of the National Stadium, honours Wint and McKenley with Rhoden and Laing, the Golden Quartet of Helsinki, 1952, 4x400m relay. 'Champs', 107 years old, running since 1910, the biggest school athletics meet in the world, the cradle of Jamaican Olympic greatness. Where will the Bolt monument go? Man of history, leading Marley and Garvey in taking this little Rock to the world.

Among his numerous awards around the world, Dr the Honourable Usain St Leo Bolt rounds out his Olympic triple triple with a triple award of Man of the Year in the 37-year-old Gleaner Honour Awards which recognises outstanding Jamaicans for their exemplary contributions in various fields. Bolt on the track. *Gleaner* 'Man of the Year', 2008, 2009, 2016. Seven-time winner of the RJR Sport Foundation 'National Sportsman of the Year': 2008, 2009, 2011, 2012, 2013, 2015, 2016.

The 183-year-old *Gleaner*, a true Jamaican icon, publishes from its archives this souvenir photo album to honour a dazzling star, a legend, unrivalled in his field, rising from among us and taking it to the world with lightning speed: 9.58.

As the Lightning Bolt exits competition, just days shy of his 31st birthday, IAAF World Championships, London, August 4–13, The Gleaner offers his fans and a proud, pleased and grateful nation, and the rest of the world which equally adores Bolt, these fine selected frames of 'The Legend', on and off the track, as a keepsake marking unmatched greatness.

'I want', 'The Legend' says about his legacy, 'to be remembered as one of the greatest athletes ever in sport…but I also want to be remembered as a laid-back, chilled, fun-loving person who inspires others.' Double mission accomplished – and exceeded!

'I want to be remembered as one of the greatest athletes ever in sport...but I also want to be remembered as a laid-back, chilled, fun-loving person who inspires others.'

Usain Bolt

PART 1:
The Making of a Legend

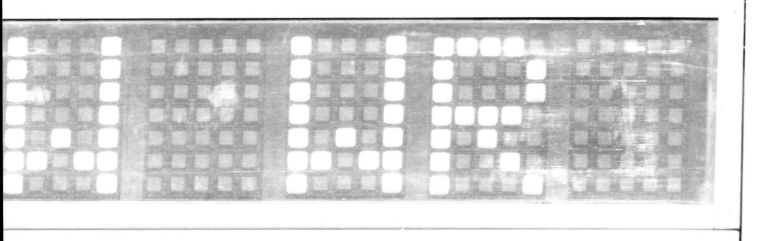

Announcing Himself to the World

In August 2008, the athletics world was struck by double 'Bolts' of lightning when Usain Bolt announced himself as the fastest man to have ever bestrode the earth as he effortlessly crossed the finish line to win the 100m and 200m at the Beijing Olympics. Not only did he decimate his rivals in a show of awesome speed never before witnessed in international competition, but in the process established new world records with such effrontery, panache and sheer *joie de vivre* that the world immediately knew someone special had arrived. Was this man-boy who was about to turn 21 for real, or were these performances a once-in-a-lifetime achievement never to be repeated or surpassed?

Over the next eight years at two succeeding Olympic Games and four World Championships, that question was answered time after time by Bolt's scintillating performances that brought excitement, glamour and new life to track and field and changed the face of the sport forever. Bolt's inexorable and relentless march to the status of 'Legend' – a title and recognition for which he shamelessly craved and tirelessly worked, was to be finally achieved by unanimous global acclaim when he achieved the impossible 'triple triple' at the Rio Olympics in 2016.

2008: THE BEIJING SUMMER OLYMPICS

In Beijing, Bolt found that chicken nuggets was the only meal he could have without a stomach upset and 'ate them fifteen at a time for breakfast, lunch and dinner washed down with bottled water'. He qualified for the 100m final with times of 9.92 and 9.85 seconds in the quarter-finals and semi-finals, respectively. His rival, Tyson Gay, got hurt in the semi-finals and was out of the race, and as he lined up for the start of the race he detected that his compatriot, Asafa Powell, seemed to be under stress. Ten metres from the finish line, Bolt was ahead. 'I threw my hands up in the air and acted all mad. I pounded my chest because I knew that nobody was going to catch me. It was done, I was the Olympic champ…' His time of 9.69 seconds established a new Olympic and world record.

The 200m was next, and the question on everyone's mind was whether he would break Michael Johnson's world record of 19.32 seconds set at the 1996

Summer Olympics in Atlanta. In his favourite event, Bolt's demolition of the opposition was even more complete, and despite a 0.9 m/s headwind, he set a new world and Olympic record of 19.30 seconds. Following the race, 'Happy Birthday' was played over the stadium's sound system and sung by 90,000 spectators in anticipation of his 22nd birthday the next day. This feat made him the first sprinter to break both records at the same Olympics.

Two days later, Bolt ran on the third leg in the Jamaican 4x100m relay team, increasing his gold medal total to three. Along with teammates Nesta Carter, Michael Frater, and Asafa Powell, Bolt broke another world and Olympic record, their 37.10 seconds finish breaking the previous mark by three-tenths of a second. The sight of Bolt running behind Asafa Powell encouraging him all the way to the world record will always be remembered.

2009 BERLIN WORLD CHAMPIONSHIPS

At the 2009 World Championships in Berlin, Bolt improved his world record with a time of 9.58 seconds to win his first World Championships gold medal. In the 200m final, Bolt broke his own record by 0.11 seconds, finishing with a time of 19.19 seconds, and with the other members of the Jamaican 4x100m relay team ran 37.31 seconds to establish a new championship record.

On the last day of the Berlin Championships, the Governing Mayor of Berlin, Klaus Wowereit, presented Bolt with a 12-foot high section of the Berlin Wall in a small

The Jamaican 4x100m relay team ran 37.31 seconds to establish a new championship record.

ceremony, saying Bolt had shown that 'one can tear down walls that had been considered as insurmountable.' The nearly three-ton segment was delivered to the Jamaica Military Museum in Kingston.

2011 DAEGU WORLD CHAMPIONSHIPS

Bolt went undefeated over 100m and 200m in the 2011 season and was automatically installed as the favourite to win both sprints at the World Championships in Daegu that year. However, tragedy struck in the 100m race. Bolt was eliminated from the final after false starting, but had the consolation of seeing his teammate Yohan Blake win the race in 9.92 seconds. This might have shattered the confidence of a lesser man but Bolt's ability to rise above adversity was demonstrated when he stormed back to capture the 200m gold medal in fine style. With this achievement, Bolt joined Calvin Smith to become the second sprinter to win consecutive 200m World titles. The climax fittingly came with another gold medal and world record performance in the 4x100m relay, when Bolt, along with Nesta Carter Michael Frater and Yohan Blake, set a world record time of 37.04 seconds.

2012 LONDON SUMMER OLYMPICS

At the 2012 London Olympics, Bolt won the 100m gold medal with a time of 9.63 seconds, to defend his gold medal from the 2008 Beijing Games. He followed this up with a successful defence of his Olympic 200m title with a time of 19.32 seconds, followed by Blake at 19.44 and Warren Weir at 19.84 to complete a Jamaican podium sweep. With this, Bolt became the first man in history to defend both the 100m and 200m Olympic sprint titles. He was dramatic in victory; in the final metres of the 200m race, Bolt placed his fingers on his lips, gesturing to silence his critics, and after crossing the line he completed five push-ups – one for each of his Olympic gold medals.

On the final day of the 2012 Olympics, Bolt participated in Jamaica's gold medal-winning 4×100m relay team along with Carter, Frater and Blake. With a time of 36.84 seconds, they knocked two tenths of a second off their previous world record from 2011.

Usain St Leo Bolt was now at the top of the sprinting world.

Usain Bolt with Berlin's Mayor Klaus Wowereit and 'his' piece of the Berlin Wall

...200m Gold!
WR 19.30 seconds

Beijing 2008 100m Gold!
WR 9.69 seconds
(even with laces untied)

...4x100m relay Gold!
WR 37.10 seconds

'I am on my way to being a legend.'

Usain Bolt after winning the double sprint title in Berlin, both in world record times.

Berlin 2009 World Championships Gold! Gold! Gold!
100m: WR 9.58 seconds
200m: WR 19.19 seconds
4x100m relay: Championship Record 37.31 seconds

As smooth as silk...

...poetry in motion

9

'For me, it was really a good run. I went out there to make up for the 100m and do something special for the fans.'

Usain Bolt after winning the 200m at the 2011 Daegu World Championships

At the 2012 London Olympics, Bolt became the first man in history to successfully defend both the 100m and 200m Olympic sprint titles.

'Usain Bolt is clearly a legend –
no one else has ever won back-
to-back 100m and 200m.'
Sebastian Coe

The clanging of 'Dutch pot' covers became a popular ritual of crowds celebrating victory by Jamaican athletes.

'I told him if he broke the national 200m record he can run a 100m. After the race he didn't even say thank you. He just said "When is the hundred?"'

Glen Mills, Usain Bolt's coach

That first 100m was in the Greek island of Crete in 2007 when Bolt was timed in 10.03 seconds for his first ever senior 100m race.

Did You Know?

Bolt broke the 100m World Record in only his second international competitive race over that distance in New York City in 2008.

The Road to Legend Status

By the 2012 London Olympics, Bolt was already acknowledged internationally as the greatest sprinter of all time, and following those Olympics, he was confirmed as the highest-earning track and field athlete in history. He had certainly eclipsed Carl Lewis and Maurice Greene but was yet to carve out that special niche reserved for legends.

2013 WORLD CHAMPIONSHIPS

In 2013, Bolt suffered one of his rare defeats in the 100m to the American Justin Gatlin in the Rome Diamond League, but went on to win the event at the Jamaica National Championships ahead of Kemar Bailey-Cole. In the run-up to the 2013 World Athletics Championships in Moscow, his fitness improved and Bolt set world-leading times in the sprints, with 9.85 seconds for the 100m at the London Anniversary Games and 19.73 for the 200m in Paris.

He regained the title as the world's fastest man by winning the World Championships 100m in Moscow, where in wet conditions he defeated Gatlin by recording 9.77 seconds, which was fastest time run that year, to Gatlin's 9.85. He was hardly challenged in the 200m final, which he won over one-tenth of a second ahead of his teammate Warren Weir in a time of 19.66 seconds. This performance made Bolt the first man in the history of the 200m at the World Championships in Athletics to win three gold medals over the distance.

By winning a third consecutive world relay gold medal in the 4×100m relay final, Bolt became the most successful athlete in the 30-year history of the World Championships. Then, with Bolt running the anchor leg, the Jamaican team, which included four of the top five from the 100m final, won the 4x100m relay three tenths of a second ahead of the American team anchored by Gatlin. For the fifth time in six years, Bolt was named IAAF World Male Athlete of the Year.

THE 2014 COMMONWEALTH GAMES

An injury to Bolt's hamstring in March 2014 caused him to miss nine weeks of training. He recovered from surgery in time to compete in the 4×100m relay of the 2014 Commonwealth Games in Glasgow. Not in peak form, Bolt said that he was attending the Games for the fans and to show his progress since the

injury. Bolt and his teammates won the 4×100m relay in 37.58 seconds to set a new Commonwealth Games record. Bolt may not have lit up the track with a scintillating individual performance, but his very presence at the Games had a major impact on Glasgow and brought new life and energy to the city and his fans. In his only individual race for 2014, Bolt set the indoor 100m world record in Warsaw with a time of 9.98 seconds.

2015 BEIJING WORLD CHAMPIONSHIPS

Coach Glen Mills considered Bolt's performance in 2015 nothing short of a miracle given the extent of his injuries that year. When he returned to the track after recovering from injury, Bolt ran only two 100m and three 200m races before the World Championships. His times of 10.12

seconds for the 100m and 20.20 seconds for the 200m seemed pedestrian, and his season's best of 20.13 seconds for the 200m ranked him 20th in the world going into the Championships.

Two 100m runs of 9.87 seconds in July in London showed that he was returning to better form, but was still below top-ranked, Justin Gatlin who had times of 9.74 and 19.57 seconds. For the first time since 2009 Bolt was not the favourite entering the World Championships to defend his sprint titles.

In the 100m, Bolt won his semi-final in 9.96 seconds, a much slower time than Gatlin's 9.77 seconds, but in the finals, against the odds Bolt demonstrated mental toughness to finish .01 second ahead of Gatlin in 9.79 seconds. Bolt repeated his victory over Gatlin in the 200m final when he ran 19.55 seconds to win followed by Gatlin in 19.74 seconds. Bolt's four consecutive wins over

200m at the World Championships were unprecedented and established him clearly as the best ever sprinter in the competition. Bolt received his fourth consecutive gold medal in the 4 × 100m relay when the Jamaica team, including Nesta Carter, Asafa Powell and Nickel Ashmeade raced to victory.

Bolt demonstrated mental toughness to finish .01 second ahead of Gatlin

2016 Rio Olympics

In the run-up to the Rio Olympics, Bolt competed in only one 200m race, the London Grand Prix, which he won in a time of 19.89 seconds. His best time in his four 100m victories before the Olympics was 9.88 seconds, which placed him fourth on the world seasonal rankings. However, despite these relatively slow times, by his standards, his mind was clearly fixed on becoming a sprinting legend. 'I want to be among greats Muhammad Ali and Pelé.'

At the 2016 Rio Olympics, Bolt won the 100m gold medal with a time of 9.81 seconds. With this achievement, he became the first athlete to win the event three times at the Olympic Games. Bolt followed up his 100m win with a gold medal in the 200m, which also makes him the first athlete to win the 200m three times at the Olympic Games. Bolt ran the anchor leg for the finals of the 4x100 m relay and secured his third consecutive and last Olympic gold medal in the event. With that win, Bolt obtained the 'triple triple', three sprinting gold medals in three consecutive Olympics, and finished his Olympic career with a 100% win record in finals.

The Legend

Even before announcing his decision to retire from athletics after the 2017 World Championships, Bolt had certainly achieved legendary status. He had joined the iconic performing artiste, Bob Marley, as the two most easily recognised Jamaicans of all time. In 2009, at age 23, he became 'The Honourable' Usain St Leo Bolt, OJ, the youngest member of the Order of Jamaica 'for outstanding performance in the field of athletics at the international level.' He was voted the Jamaica Sportsman of the Year in 2008, 2009, 2011, 2012 and 2013.

To the extent that a social process can be represented by an individual, Bolt had transformed athletics and given the sport a new dynamic. His international awards include:

- IAAF World Athlete of the Year: 2008, 2009, 2011, 2012, 2013, 2016
- Track & Field Athlete of the Year: 2008, 2009
- Laureus World Sportsman of the Year: 2009, 2010, 2013 and 2016
- BBC Overseas Sports Personality of the Year: 2008, 2009, 2012
- L'Équipe Champion of Champions: 2008, 2009, 2012, 2015

Bolt is one of only nine athletes to win World Championships gold at the youth, junior, and senior levels of an athletic event. His eight Olympic and 11 World Championships gold medals finally confirmed his own assessment of his career:

'I could call myself a sporting legend.'

World champion in the 100m and 200m in Moscow 2013, Bolt became the first man in the history of the 200m at the World Championships to win three gold medals over this distance.

Bolt demonstrated mental toughness to win the 100m against all odds at the 2015 World Championships in Beijing

'There was never any doubt for me that I would win my 200m.'

Usain Bolt

LEGEND!!
'I don't need to prove anything else. What else do I need to prove to the world that I am the greatest?'

Usain Bolt after achieving the 'triple triple' at the 2016 Rio Olympics

'I am never disappointed in anything I do. I have proven myself to the world, I have done great things, I have come back now from injury, I am not stressed. I still have the world records…I am happy.'

Usain Bolt after the 2016 Rio Olympics

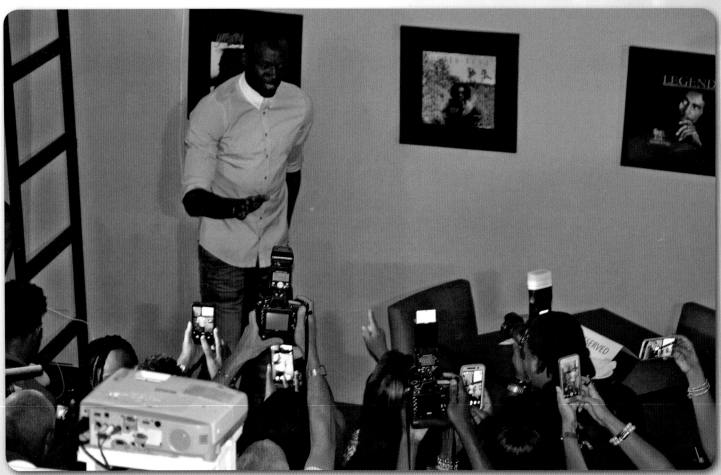

Did You Know?

Usain has a habit of not cutting or grooming his hair for World Championships.

Bolt by the Numbers

Simply put, Usain Bolt is the best sprinter of all time. Thirteen individual gold medals, seven at the World Championships and six at the Olympic Games, are the stuff of legends. Add five individual world records, with four of them set in major finals, and his claim to a rare level of greatness becomes undeniable.

There are fascinating numbers behind the honours listed above. When you sift through them, they amaze you at first. Then they hit home with the confirmation of Bolt's top sprinter status.

FASTEST FIVE

His compatriot Asafa Powell broke 10 seconds on 98 occasions having long overtaken the tally of 51 such races by American Maurice Greene. Bolt comes next with 49 sub-10 seconds.

As you might have guessed, the tall man from Trelawny is supreme at the sharp end of the list. He has 12 runs under 9.80 seconds, three of the fastest five and the two fastest of all, his world record of 9.58 seconds at the 2009 World Championships in Berlin and his Olympic record 9.63 seconds from the 2012 final in London.

He shares the third fastest time – 9.69 seconds which was a world record when he ran it to win the 2008 Beijing Olympics – with Tyson Gay and Yohan Blake. His 9.69 seconds came in his fourth race in two days in Beijing, while Gay and Blake scored theirs in one-off races in Shanghai and Lausanne, respectively.

The average of Bolt's 10 fastest 100m races is 9.73. Only Gay, Blake, Powell and Bolt himself have ever gone quicker than that.

YOUR BENCHMARK

Although only two of his individual world records have come in the 200m, he is far better in this event than anyone else. He has broken 20 seconds 34 times, 10 clear of Namibia's Frank Fredericks and 11 ahead of the American pair of superman Michael Johnson and Wallace Spearmon, who have 23 each.

If you grew up with the 1968 world record of 19.83 seconds by Tommie Smith as your benchmark, Bolt's numbers will blow you away. He has run under

19.80 seconds 21 times, with 14 of those under 19.70 seconds. Nine of the 16 clockings under 19.60 seconds and five of the seven under 19.50 seconds were run by Bolt.

If that weren't enough, he is the only athlete to have broken 20 seconds while still a junior athlete. He did it twice. The first one is the World Junior record of 19.93 at the 2004 CARIFTA Games. That spellbinding run in Bermuda broke his tie with American Roy Martin, who had the old mark at 20.13 seconds.

Bolt's top ten 200m times average out to 19.47 seconds. Other than the man himself, only Blake and Johnson have dipped under that threshold. It's amazing.

Fast When it Counts

It's an understatement to say Bolt is good in big meets. From 2008 onwards, he has produced his best times of each season in major finals. Most of us remember his world records in Beijing in 2008 and in Berlin the following year, but he never stopped speeding. Days after his shocking false start in the 100m at the 2011 World Championships, he stormed home in the 200m in 19.40 seconds, then the 4th fastest of all time. At the London Olympics, he pulled out his best runs of 2012 with the second fastest 100m of all time – 9.63 seconds – and a clocking of 19.32 seconds in the 200m despite an aching back. His times have been more modest since. Still, at the 2013 and 2015 World Championships and the 2016 Olympics, his winning times have been his best efforts in all those seasons.

Bringing the Best Out of Others

Bolt's rivals have raised their game to keep up. From Richard Thompson of Trinidad and Tobago in the 2008 Olympic 100m to Canadian Andre De Grasse in the 2016 Olympics, sprinters have produced personal bests galore to stay close. The chart lists them all, but Anaso Jobodwana may be the athlete who revs the most when he races Bolt. The South African did a personal best of 20.27 seconds in Bolt's 2012 Olympic 200m semi-final and 20.12 seconds a year later at the World Championships.

With Bolt inspiring him to speed, Jobodwana zipped along in 20.01 seconds in the 2015 World Championships semi-final won by Bolt and then 19.87 seconds in the final where Bolt's winning time was 19.55 seconds.

'Losing to Bolt is kinda like winning the race to everyone else.'

Richard Thompson, Trinidad and Tobago
Beijing 2008 Olympics 100m Silver medallist

PULLED TO PERSONAL BESTS BY BOLT?

2008 OLYMPICS
100m

2.	Richard Thompson	TTO	9.89
3.	Walter Dix	USA	9.91
4.	Churandy Martina	AHO	9.93

2009 WORLD CHAMPIONSHIPS
100m

2.	Tyson Gay	USA	9.71

200m

2.	Alonso Edward	Panama	19.81
4.	Steve Mullings	Jamaica	19.98

2011 WORLD CHAMPIONSHIPS
200m

3.	Christophe Lemaitre	France	19.80

2012 OLYMPICS
100m

2.	Yohan Blake (equals personal best)	Jamaica	9.75
3.	Justin Gatlin	USA	9.80
5.	Ryan Bailey	USA	9.88

200m

3.	Warren Weir	Jamaica	19.84

Semi-finals

2.	Anaso Jobodwana	SA	20.27
4.	Aaron Brown	Canada	20.42

2013 WORLD CHAMPIONSHIPS
200m

2.	Warren Weir	Jamaica	19.79

Semi-finals

2.	Anaso Jobodwana	SA	20.13

Heats

8.	Didier Kiki	Benin	22.01

2015 WORLD CHAMPIONSHIPS
100m

3.	Andre De Grasse	Canada	9.92

Semi-finals

	Bingtan Su	China	9.99

200m

3.	Anaso Jobodwana	SA	19.87
5.	Zharnel Hughes	GB	20.02

Semi-finals

2.	Anaso Jobodwana	SA	20.01
6.	Danny Talbot	GB	20.27

2016 OLYMPICS
100m

3.	Andre De Grasse	Canada	9.91
6.	Ben Meite	Ivory Coast	9.96

Semi-finals

2.	Andre De Grasse	Canada	9.92

200M
Semi-finals

2.	Andre De Grasse	Canada	19.80

Heats

2.	Ejo Oduduru	Nigeria	20.34

It is perhaps a stretch to reason that Bolt makes his opponents set personal bests when they race him. After all, every world-class athlete trains to be in peak form on the days that count the most. However, it seems clear that Bolt's world records in 2008 opened an era where his rivals had to summon a higher level of performance to stand a chance.

FAST AT HOME AND ABROAD

In 2008 and 2010, Bolt laid down the best times on local soil in the 100m and 200m, respectively. At the 2008 Jamaica Invitational, he rushed through the 100m in 9.76 seconds, which was just 0.02 off Powell's then world record. Two years later at the same meet, he thrilled a sell-out crowd inside the National Stadium running the 200m in 19.56 seconds.

His overseas fans have had their fair share of his lightning speed. Bolt has the fastest 100m times ever run in New York, Beijing and Berlin, the three cities where he broke the world record, as well as in Brussels, Moscow, Saint-Denis and Oslo.

The 9.69-second clockings by Blake and Gay place them ahead of Bolt in Lausanne and Shanghai.

In the 200m, Bolt is the quickest ever in Berlin and Beijing, where he set world records, and in London, Daegu, Lausanne, Zurich, Moscow, Athens and Thessaloniki.

WHICH IS BOLT'S BETTER EVENT?

Bolt has only two world records in the 200m compared to three in the 100m. His best times in each event are both brilliant – 9.58 seconds for the 100m and 19.19 seconds in the sprint once known as the 'deuce'. The IAAF Comparison Tables, designed to help rank performances in different track and field events, provide a split decision. The 100m world record earns 1,356 points while the 200m world mark gets 1,351 points.

The tables turn when Bolt's top 10 average times are put under the microscope. His 100m top ten average is 9.73 seconds and that collects 1,301 points. The corresponding figure for the 200m – 19.47 – takes 13.05 points from the IAAF Comparison Tables.

If you view the average as a measure of how fast he has been continuously, the 200m is just ahead.

That is confirmed by an analysis of his comparative win-loss records from 2008 onwards. You can count his 100m losses on one had with a finger to spare. Powell, Gay, Blake and Justin Gatlin are the elite group to have beaten him in the 100m, and none of them has done it twice. For the 200m, you only need one finger. His loss to Blake at the

2012 National Senior Championships is the only blemish on his competitive record in the period starting in 2008.

Finally, he has won more World and Olympic medals in the 2008–2016 period in the longer race. He blotted his copybook with a shocking false start in the 100m final of the 2011 World Championships. There has been no such lapse in the 200m where he has three Olympic gold medals and four World Championship gold medals. By comparison, he is 3 and 3 in the 100m at the Olympics and the Worlds.

He did win his first major medal in the 200m, a silver behind Gay at the 2007 Worlds, but that was a year before he took up the 100m as a

championship distance. Of course, he is the long-range favourite to bring his World 100m gold medal count up to four this year. Sadly, he is not planning to run the 200m.

When you roll the times, the averages, the win-loss record and the medal count together, the conclusion stares you in the face. He is better at 200m. It is as simple as B-O-L-T.

INDOORS

It's probably been wise for the 6 ft 5" Bolt never to have run indoors. Instead, he has often used the first quarter of the year to run 400m races and relays. Still, the curious mind sometimes wonders how he would fare if he ventured under cover. The only clue comes from a statistical breakdown of his 100m world record released by the IAAF. It turns out that Bolt covered the first 60m in 6.32 seconds. Maurice Greene, 100m Olympic champion in 2000 and three-time World champion, holds the world record for the indoor 60m at 6.39 seconds. The Jamaican record is 6.44 held by Powell.

BEST OF ALL TIME

It's hard to compare athletics from different eras. The great Americans Jesse Owens and Bob Hayes raced at a time when professional careers in athletics weren't common and so very few American men did more than one Olympics. Owens came to fame when he set or equalled six world records in one day in 1935. That magnificent day of days contained a record-equalling run in

'Usain made me better because he has forced me and other sprinters to change the way we think.'

Tyson Gay

the 100 yards and new marks in the 220 yards, long jump, the 220-yard low hurdles. When his great runs in the 220-yard races were converted to metres, he had touched two world records there as well. He won four gold medals to be the star of the 1936 Games, but couldn't have gone to another Olympics even if he wanted. The Second World War forced the cancellation of the 1940 and 1944 Olympics.

Hayes, the dominant sprinter of the early sixties, concentrated on the 100m at the 1964 Olympic Games in Tokyo, won it in the world record time of 10.06 seconds, but then departed to a successful career in American football.

Carl Lewis won four gold medals at the 1984 Games and, like Owens, was a long jumper in addition to being a 100m and 200m sprinter. Bolt has always concentrated on the dashes.

Lewis, Greene and Bolt each have three World 100m titles but Lewis won his in 1983, 1987 and 1991, with a world record of 9.86 seconds as the cherry topping on his hat-trick, when the World Championships were held every four years. From then onward, athletes have had the opportunity to become World Champion every two years. Greene won his 100m crowns in 1997, 1999, when he did the sprint double, and in 2001.

There is, nevertheless, a point of comparison which separates Bolt from the illustrious trio of Owens, Hayes and Lewis. The tall Jamaican won both his 2008 Olympic 100m and 200m gold medals in world record times. No other male sprinter has ever done that, but that shouldn't be a surprise.

After all, there has never been a sprinter quite like Bolt.

'If you have been following me since 2002, you would know I have been doing phenomenal things since I was 15. I was the youngest person to win the World Juniors. I won the World Youth record at 17. I've broken every record there is in every event I have ever done…I'm just living out my dream now. I was always going to be great.'

Usain Bolt

*The first of many: Kingston 2002
World Junior Champion*

'You have Einstein.
You have Isaac Newton.
You have Beethoven.
You have Usain Bolt.
You have people who
are exceptions. It is not
explainable how and what
they do.'
Stephen Francis, coach of
the MVP Track Club, Jamaica

Did You Know?

Bolt and the USA's Wallace Spearmon are close friends off the track although sharing a keen rivalry on the track.

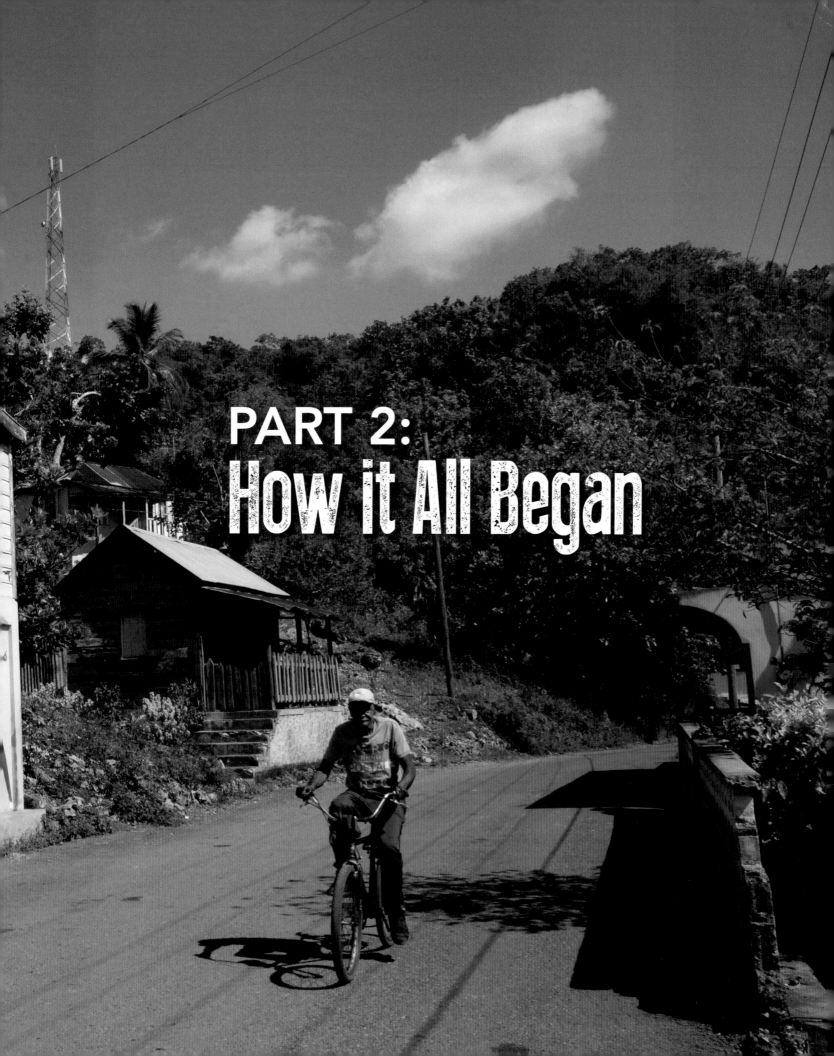

PART 2:
How it All Began

Roots - Sherwood Content

Who could have guessed that the bauxite boom in the 1950s would have a profound influence on not only Jamaica's track and field history but the world as well?

Wellesley Bolt, the father of now eight-time Olympic champion Usain Bolt, is originally from Alexandria in St Ann. As fate would have it, the Bolts were living on bauxite-rich lands, and when the big companies came calling in the early to mid-1950s they were moved from their St Ann roots and resettled in the parish of Trelawny in an area close to the world-famous Windsor Caves. Usain's mother is a native of Trelawny and is originally from a district known as Reserve, an area very close to Sherwood Content where the Bolts now reside. In fact, the world's fastest man grew up in an offshoot of Sherwood Content, a district known as Cox Heath. Bolt's first school was Piedmont Basic, up to age six, before he moved to Waldensia Primary, the school which both his mother and father attended in earlier years.

While many interesting stories have been told about his early life, Usain Bolt was not a superstar from birth. As he has said himself, it took very hard work to get to the top of world sprinting. 'As a young boy he was mainly a cricketer and he also played football,' his manager and mentor, Norman Peart, says, 'At primary school everybody ran on sports day. In grades five and six he started to show some talent. He ran against bigger boys and beat them. He went to the Jamaica Teachers' Association (JTA)-Blue Cross meet for primary schools and did very well.' At primary school, local Baptist pastor and teacher at Waldensia, Devere Nugent, was the first to spot that Bolt had real talent at the school's sports day. 'His primary school coach knew him as a cricketer but saw the talent when he ran on sports day,' Peart said. 'While preparing for the Blue Cross meet he gave him his first coaching lessons.' Coaches from the top schools were at the Blue Cross meet, all seeking to recruit the best talent and Bolt was one of those who was spotted. Young Bolt did nothing earth-shattering but his mother remembers that Clarendon-based Vere Technical High School tried to recruit the future star.

Neither Usain nor his parents wanted a separation from his quiet surroundings in Trelawny and when he sat his Grade Six Achievement Test (GSAT) examinations for entry to secondary school, William Knibb Memorial High in Falmouth was the only choice. Then principal at William Knibb, Margaret Lee, was, according to Peart, someone who saw the value of sports in the development of the school. 'She was a sports enthusiast and would have got word that this (Bolt) was a good one,' Peart said.

His first coach at William Knibb was Pablo McNeil. McNeil, who died in 2011, was an Olympic sprinter who represented Jamaica at the Tokyo Games in 1964 and in Mexico City four years later. He had the experience at the top level and would have left his mark on the young Bolt. McNeil retired and left after Class Three, but was later brought back to the school to assist the then coach Dwight Barnett. That was in 2002 and Bolt was ready to explode. Earlier, in grades eight and nine, Bobby Brown and Darlon Clarke were two who helped to lay the foundation for his track career.

Barnett, now coaching at St Catherine High School, guided Bolt during his most successful years at the GraceKennedy-ISSA Boys and Girls' Championships. He began working with Bolt in 2001 and remembers him as a jovial but extremely confident athlete. 'He was much then like he is now. We had to be strict with him at times to ensure that he stayed on the right path,' Barnett said. 'But whenever he was competing he was very confident. He always wanted to win.'

In Class Three at 'Champs', Bolt was a short sprinter, 100 and 200m, but Barnett and his staff changed that. 'When we looked at his height, we thought the 200 and 400m would be the two best events for him,' according to Barnett.

'When you were around Usain Bolt and saw him, both at training and on the track competing, you immediately knew there was something special about him.'

Bolt began performing consistently well in 2002 and Barnett said he began to 'win everything' starting with the development meets, Boys Championships and later at the IAAF World Junior Championships at the National Stadium where he was the undoubted star. Even before those performances on the junior world stage Barnett knew he had a gem in his hands. 'When you were around Usain Bolt and saw him, both at training and on the track competing, you immediately knew there was something special about him. When I went with him to the various meets and at the IAAF World Youth Championships in 2003, I realised that he was not a normal athlete. He would dominate and was far ahead of the other athletes.' Peart, himself a Trelawny native and tax auditor who began helping Bolt with his school work in 2002, still remembers him as one who trained very hard each day before going home. 'Nobody was close to him; he had no real mentors. In track and field, he looked up to Herb McKenley,' Peart said.

Much has been made of the fact that Bolt comes from 'yam country' in Trelawny. However Peart revealed that fresh cow's milk was a big part of Bolt's early diet. 'His grandfather reared cows and he drank lots of milk. At a young age his grandfather took fresh cow's milk for him every day and he really looked forward to that.'

Like most rural dwellers, Bolt was a regular church-goer as a young boy. He grew up in the Seventh-day Adventist Church, which was his mother's denomination. Although Bolt remains faithful to his religious upbringing, Peart says he does not attend church as regularly as when he was a teen.

'We used to run too. I used to run the 200 and 400m, and his father, too, but none of us was so fast in our time. We're not surprised that he is doing so well because he puts everything into it.'

Jennifer Bolt, July 2002

'His speed ratio from then, at William Knibb, satisfied me
that he was the best and was going to demolish the world.'

The late Pablo McNeil, Jamaican Olympian and
Bolt's first coach at William Knibb Memorial High School

While he belongs to all Jamaicans, he is first and foremost a son of the community of Sherwood Content.

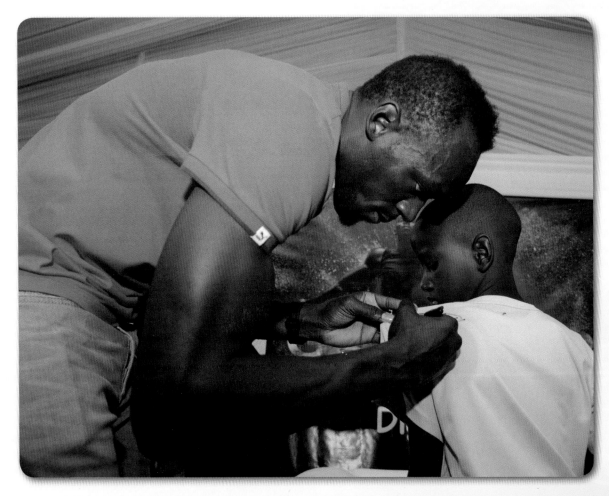

Norman Peart (centre), Bolt's business manager has been associated with him since 2002 when he began helping Bolt with his schoolwork.

Bolt Beginnings: 'Champs'

Those who watched the incomparable Usain Bolt striding to 13 individual gold medals at the Olympics and World Championships might be surprised at the modest start to his Boys and Girls' Championships career. Empty-handed after his first trip to the storied high school championships, he had but one single silver medal after his second 'Champs'.

In 2000, the gangly student athlete from William Knibb Memorial High School strode home in fifth place in the Class Three 200m final. He was eight-tenths away from the gold medal won by Keith Spence of Cornwall College. Bolt, whose speed had been seen on the cricket pitch, had a long way to go.

Coached by 1964 Olympic sprinter Pablo McNeil, the tall boy got his first 'Champs' medal in 2001. He was a strong second in 22.04 seconds in the 200m as Tesfa Latty of St George's College completed the 100m and 200m sprint double in his school's 150th anniversary year.

Boys and Girls' Championships was a strange affair in 2002. With the National Stadium closed for the laying of a new track in anticipation of the IAAF World Junior Championships, 'Champs' was shunted to the GC Foster College for Physical Education.

Spectators were few, but those who were there saw Bolt dazzle. He won the Class Two 400m easily in 47.4 seconds and might have broken the record had it not been for a power failure which stopped the electronic timer during the race and protected the mark of 47.49 set by Edward Clarke of Jamaica College in 1991. Bolt duly equalled Latty's 200m record to complete the double.

Now 15, the speedy stripling improved after 'Champs' and lowered his 200m personal best to 20.58 seconds before the World Juniors. On the new track inside the refurbished National Stadium, Bolt won Jamaica's only individual World Junior gold medal in 20.61 seconds and added relay silver in both the 4x100 and 4x400m.

He arrived at 'Champs' 2003 as a star and did not disappoint. With Dwight Barnett now directing his training, Bolt first destroyed the Class One 400m record with a searing run of 45.35 seconds. Sadly, Jermaine Gonzales, the defending champion from Tacius Golding High School, fell to injury just as he was summoning a strong finish in response to Bolt's lightning-fast start.

That race took place under overcast skies and with an accompanying drizzle.

The gloom was replaced by bright sunshine when Bolt settled into the blocks for what became his last race at 'Champs', the Class One 200m final. It was an exuberant show of speed that ended just 20.25 seconds after the gun was fired. His 400m record has since been broken and surpassed by Javon Francis and Akeem Bloomfield, but the 200m mark that had fans chanting his name still stands in 2017, 14 years later.

In 2004, David Hunt, author of the *Champs Preview*, wrote,

> ***Everytime he graced the track, spectators immediately rose to their feet, anticipating something special from a special athlete. Bolt did not disappoint, and his record-breaking runs in the Class One 400 and 200 left the National Stadium buzzing with excitement long after the races had been completed.***

He finished the year by equalling the long-standing World Junior 200m record of 20.13 seconds at the Pan-Am Junior Championships in Barbados and with gold at the World Youth Championships. A memorable moment came at the National Senior Championships when he beat his elders, including 2001 World Championships silver medal winner Chris Williams, all handily.

He had enough in reserve that he could salute the National Stadium fans at the finish.

Bolt winning the 200m race at 'Champs' 2003 in a record time of 20.25, which as at 2017, still stands.

Greeted by Olympian Juliet Cuthbert and below in
a contemplative mood with close friend and rival
Jermaine Gonzales.

Congratulated by proud mother Jennifer Bolt after
winning 200m gold at the World Juniors in 2002.

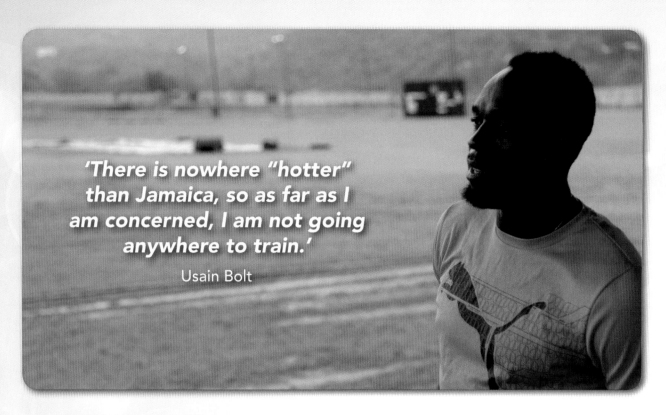

'There is nowhere "hotter" than Jamaica, so as far as I am concerned, I am not going anywhere to train.'

Usain Bolt

Racers Track Club has been a home to Bolt since 2005 when Glen Mills took over as his coach. The club has nurtured scores of Jamaica's Olympians and World Championships athletes, including Bolt.

From one champion to another: Bolt with South African 400m Olympic champion Wayde Van Niekerk at Racers training in Kingston.

Bolt, Nugent Walker and Anna 'Tannie Anns' Botha, coach of Wayde Van Niekerk

Racing for Racers

Racers Track Club hosts an annual Award of Excellence ceremony as well as its Grand Prix athletics meet which attracts world-renowned athletes. The 2017 staging was a tribute to Bolt and witnessed his last competitive race in Jamaica before his official retirement from international track and field.

Did You Know?

Much has been made of Trelawny yam as the secret factor in Bolt's success, but could it also have been the fresh cow's milk provided by his grandfather, which was an important part of his early diet?

From Disappointments to the Top of the World

olt's potential had not gone unnoticed. Then president of the Jamaica Athletics Administrative Association (JAAA) Neville 'Teddy' McCook had mapped out a development plan for him. Bolt left William Knibb and 'Champs' two years early and went to Kingston into the care of veteran coach, Fitz Coleman at the High Performance Centre located at the University of Technology (UTech).

The new partnership had spectacular results. Bolt took sole ownership of the World Junior 200m record at the 2004 CARIFTA Games with a blistering run of 19.93 seconds. Twelve seasons have passed since that mind-boggling run in Bermuda and he is still the only junior to have broken 20 seconds for the event. Bolt had shared the old mark with American Roy Martin, who had clocked 20.13 seconds in 1985.

Track and Field News, the respected US magazine, suggested that he might have an outside shot at an Olympic medal in Athens, but disaster struck when Bolt suffered an injury, missed the Jamaican National Senior Championships and a possible defence of his World Junior title. He was nevertheless selected for the Olympic team. Fit but not sharp, he was eliminated in the first round. In its October 2004 edition, *Track and Field News* listed him among those who had competed at the Olympics at less than 100% fitness. It is quite likely that the injury was abetted by a curvature of Bolt's spine – a condition that has been a perennial source of woe throughout his career.

In spite of the discomforts, the year 2004 was a qualified success. No one ran the 200m faster than Bolt except Olympic champion Shawn Crawford of the US, who clocked 19.79 seconds in the finals. Bolt was six years younger and no one knew then that he would succeed the American as Olympic champion.

In 2005, Usain Bolt took perhaps the most far-reaching decision of his athletics career when he chose Glen Mills as his coach. Bolt quickly established an easy relationship with Mills and later commented, 'Immediately there was dialogue and I liked his style. He was friendly, smart and open...listened and when we spoke he explained everything to me.' Coach Glen Mills had been working to correct major defects in Bolt's sprinting technique. 'His head was back, his shoulders were well behind his centre of gravity, which resulted in him spending too much time in the air and overstriding.' By 2007, Bolt had become the first athlete over 6 ft 3" tall to develop a sprinting technique and start, which up until then was not conceived as possible for an athlete of that height.

In 2006, Bolt's first year with Mills, he set a new personal best of 19.88 seconds for the 200m, won the bronze medal at the IAAF World Athletics Final in Stuttgart, Germany, with a time of 20.10 seconds, and the silver medal at the IAAF World Cup in Athens, Greece, in a time of 19.96 seconds. In 2007, he ran 19.75 seconds in the 200m at the

Jamaican Championships to break the 36-year-old Jamaican record held by Don Quarrie. That year, Bolt ran his first international 100m race at the 23rd Vardinoyiannia meeting in Rethymno, Crete, where he set a personal best of 10.03 seconds to win the gold medal. Then at the 2007 World Championships in Osaka, Japan, he won a silver medal in the 200m in 19.91 seconds, finishing behind Tyson Gay, the leading US sprinter, who set a new Championships record with a time of 19.76 seconds. Bolt was also a member of the silver-medal winning relay team with Asafa Powell, Marvin Anderson, and Nesta Carter in the 4×100m relay. Jamaica set a national record of 37.89 seconds.

Bolt continued to develop in the 100m, and at the Jamaica Invitational in Kingston on May 3, 2008, he ran a time of 9.76 seconds. This was the second-fastest time for the event for which his countryman, Asafa Powell, held the world record of 9.74 seconds. The breakthrough came on May 31, 2008 at the Reebok Grand Prix held in the Icahn Stadium in New York City, where he ran 9.72 seconds to defeat Tyson Gay and break the world record. He was just as awesome in the 200m, with a world-leading time in Ostrava, then breaking the national record for the second time with a 19.67-second finish in Athens, Greece. Bolt was clearly ready for the 2008 Summer Olympics in Beijing and announced his decision to run both the 100m and 200m.

'He just has amazing speed for his height. Usually, that kind of speed is related to people of shorter stature.'

Coach Glen Mills

'It is a good combination, fast car, fast person.
At track and field we do it and we love it.'
Usain Bolt

'Looking for tears? Not going to happen. I'm OK.'
Usain Bolt after 100m false start at 2011 Daegu World Championships

'Glen is like a father figure to me...he has shown me the way to improve myself both as a person and as an athlete.'

Usain Bolt

Fitz Coleman, Bolt's coach at the High
Performance Centre, University of Technology

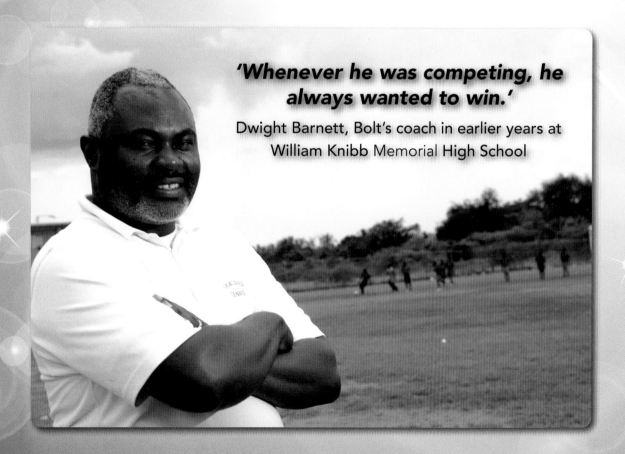

'Whenever he was competing, he always wanted to win.'

Dwight Barnett, Bolt's coach in earlier years at William Knibb Memorial High School

'He was running some phenomenal times before he was even 15. I have never shown him my stopwatch, lest it got to his head.'

The late Pablo McNeil, Jamaican Olympian and
Bolt's first coach at William Knibb Memorial High School

Did You Know?

Bolt is the only man to hold both junior and senior 200m records – 19.93 and 19.19 seconds, respectively.

PART 3:
Who Is This Man,
Usain Bolt?

Bolt: The Showman

If there was a specific moment in which Usain Bolt stopped being a mere mortal athlete and became a sporting god, it was probably his chest-thumping 'look-at-me-now' 100-metre record-setting victory at the 2008 Beijing Olympics.

Bolt, already the world-record holder in the distance, and the favourite to win the event, declared to the world in that moment of very public self-adulation on the Asian continent that he was not only physically superior to his competitors – he was also supremely confident, and not afraid to show it.

Since then, Bolt's pre-race, post-race and, yes, sometimes during-the-race antics have helped to catapult the Jamaican into the stratosphere where few other sporting greats dwell. It could be argued, in fact, that with the physical dominance Bolt has exhibited over the years, his races are often pre-determined events. Bolt will win, sure, yet every race he runs is a sold-out event. It's because the people come to see him – Bolt, the performer who is sure to do something entertaining on the track, aside from winning his race, of course.

There is a buzz in every stadium as soon as he enters. When the introductions of the athletes begin, the anticipation grows. Jamaicans at home or at gathering spots like Half-Way Tree and Cross Roads get excited. All over the world, his fans watching on TV screens of varying sizes with coverage in various languages wait to see the great man. What will Bolt do when it's his time to be introduced? The cameras turn to the 6 ft 5" sprinter and the stadium erupts. People across the globe cheer. The Bolt performance begins.

He has switched it up over the years. There was that time in Beijing when, before the race, he appeared to be checking out his new haircut, turning his head from side to side while looking at his image in the stadium monitors. In need of a shave? Bolt will surely run his hands over his growing beard, then give a shake of the head and shrug as if to acknowledge his less-than-pristine facial hair situation.

A rainy race day? Bolt mimes opening an umbrella even as he stands in the rain getting drenched. The crowd eats it up with glee.

At the 2012 Olympics in London, Bolt did one of his most memorable and talked-about moves. In the land of Queen Elizabeth, he gave a measured royal wave while being introduced before the 200m finals. Cupping his palms, Bolt gestured to the crowded stadium the way the queen acknowledges her subjects. The cheers got louder. Cameras flashed. Bolt can do no wrong.

Then, there is the dancing. On some occassions, when apparently feeling particularly joyful, Bolt is known to break into moves with questionable expertise. What he lacks in rhythm, however, he certainly makes up for in sheer enthusiasm. One of the first times he did this was his 'Nuh Linga' performance after his 200-metre victory in Beijing, which thrilled local dancehall fans. Here was one of their own on the biggest stage on earth proudly shimmying with authentic Jamaican swagger – taking local culture 'to di world' like no other Jamaican since Bob Marley had done.

As much as the people love seeing Bolt enjoy these moments of levity before and after his races, the sprinter himself appears to feed off these antics. He has said in interviews that he uses these moments to clear his mind and calm his nerves.

It appears, then, that these performances are a victory for Bolt – and his fans – even before the race is run.

'Of course, I will give him a few pointers on what it is
like to be a world-class track and field athlete.'

Usain Bolt with Britain's Prince Harry

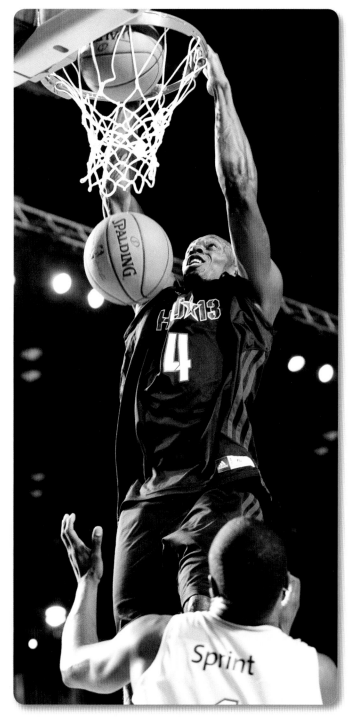

Bolt's top 10 200m times average out at 19.47 seconds. Only Yohan Blake and Michael Johnson have ever run as fast, even in an individual race.

`To di World´

It has been called the 'To di World'; the 'Lightning Bolt'; and simply the 'Bolt pose'. Whatever you call it, it's a hit. Bolt's signature pose strikes at the very heart of his competitors. The move, created with feet apart, back slightly bent while leaning to one side and pointing two index fingers to the heavens, mimics an archer preparing to launch a deadly attack – a fitting gesture for a man who reliably annihilates the competition with remarkable ease.

The pose is like a work of art – subject to many interpretations. Some, primarily those who dub the pose the 'To di World', say the gesture signifies Bolt's intention to take Jamaica to the world stage. His world-beating performances break down all barriers, and the pose, often made minutes after a race victory, is Bolt's way of symbolising the effects his performances have on placing Jamaica at the forefront of global attention.

Others say he is simply mimicking an archer to show that he wipes out his competitors with precision and impunity.

But, does the origin or intent of the pose matter at this point? The Bolt pose has become so famous that anywhere it's done it is now immediately associated with the lanky Jamaican spinter. And many persons, including stars from other sports, have taken notice.

Brazilian football great Neymar has often spoken publicly about his admiration for Bolt, and, on more than one occasion, he did the pose after scoring a goal – a homage, he said, to his sprinting hero.

After the 2016 US presidential elections, there was a lottery draw for office space at the Capitol Building in Washington, DC, for new members of Congress. The numbers drawn in the lottery by the new members would correspond with the order in which they would be allowed to choose their new offices. When Maryland Democrat Anthony Brown drew number 34 – a coveted selection – he celebrated by doing the Bolt pose.

When President Barack Obama visited Jamaica in 2015, the leader of the free world met the superstar sprinter on the campus of the University of the West Indies at Mona, and together they did the famous Bolt pose as cameras flashed and video rolled.

When Britain's Prince Harry visited Jamaica in 2012 he ran a mock race with Bolt before taking photos with the sprinter – the two of them doing the Bolt pose. That image, within minutes, appeared on websites across the world.

Bolt is a *bona fide* global icon. His signature pose is to him what shouting 'I'm the greatest!' was for boxing legend Muhammad Ali. It's his personal stamp of utter dominance – a sort of exclamation mark at the end of his awe-inspiring performances.

It's not clear if Bolt carefully planned the pose or if it simply happened in a moment of exuberance. What is without doubt, however, is that the Bolt signature pose has evolved into one of the most recognisable symbols of excellence and Jamaican sporting dominance.

Whether it was intended this way or not, this has surely taken Jamaica 'To di World'.

'The gimmicks that I do are just to make me relax. When I get to the line, it makes me relax and not worry.'

Usain Bolt

'Everything is right with me and Blake. He is the future of Jamaica.'

Usain Bolt

Did You Know?

Nugent Walker, Bolt's trusted executive manager, is also his boyhood friend.

Usain Bolt: Big Man, Big Heart

His generosity was so deep and his renown as a giver so well established that the police had to advise him to quit as it was literally causing fights at the university field where he trains!

Nugent Walker, Bolt's manager and childhood friend, reveals that Usain often travelled with a large stash of cash to training at the University of the West Indies racetrack – not to gamble (would anyone bet against him in races?) but to give away to people who would gather at trackside seeking financial favours. Bolt was only too willing to oblige. This practice became difficult to control and began to cause conflict among would-be beneficiaries as they jostled for Bolt's largesse. It was only when the police advised Bolt and his management team that the athlete's magnanimity was a source of brewing conflict that he was forced to tone down the practice.

However, it was also a security concern for Walker and the police for Bolt to be walking around with so much cash. It is said that one Christmas, he distributed the equivalent of US$30,000 in this manner to various supplicants.

It is not difficult to see why Bolt has such a heart of compassion. He grew up in rural Jamaica, born to simple, humble parents who did not have much. His father operated a village shop but was by no means a successful businessman, and as is the common practice, many people took goods on credit. From an early age then, Usain saw the deep financial needs of people – including his own parents. One of his early wishes, for instance, was to buy his mother some simple things like a washing machine for the home. So even though he hated the rigorous training regime, his early motivation to be disciplined and to buckle down to be able to do well and so help his mother, especially, was a driving force.

Usain knows what it feels like to want things that you can't afford. Hence, his early-life experience has given him a natural empathy towards those in need. His Usain Bolt Foundation has been the primary instrument through which he gives back. At his Piedmont Basic School, Usain has provided all students and teachers with physical education gear. He also underwrote the cost of the electrical rewiring of the school.

Children are very special to him and they have been the focus of his philanthropy. He has contributed significantly to the Bustamante Hospital for Children as well as to the Alpha Boys' Home. He has also contributed to the Mustard Seed Communities, which has a strong programme of assistance to children. United Way, which also has a strong focus on children, has been another important vehicle for his charitable activities.

And, of course, there is his *alma mater*, William Knibb Memorial High School. There he has built a multi-purpose playing field, and contributed to completing the construction of a lunch room and library, as well as donated significant sums of money. In his community of Sherwood Content, Trelawny, he has contributed to the Type 1 health facility as well as the Sherwood Content Health Centre.

But Usain's contribution goes beyond what he himself or his foundation donates. By insisting that all his photo shoots are to be done in Jamaica, he ensures that money goes into the pockets of ordinary Jamaicans. 'When we started out, people always wanted to do the shoots in Miami, Los Angeles and all over the world,'

Bolt is quoted as saying. But he insisted that such photo shoots, which on a typical weekend provided employment for as many as 200 people, had to be done in Jamaica. On these shoots the minimum wage earned for being just an 'extra' for six hours was US$150 which in the Jamaican context represents a very good day's pay. 'Any contract we sign has to have it clearly stated that the shoot must be done in Jamaica once the equipment is here. So we give people jobs and help many people. Many times they will come up to me and say, "big up Usain, you have really helped us by bringing the jobs here."'

"...big up Usain, you have really helped us by bringing the jobs here."

Usain has his Jamaican people at the forefront of his mind. His love is displayed in his philanthropic activities, his natural large-heartedness and in his insistence that Jamaicans participate as much as possible in his success.

He is 'The gift that keeps on giving.'

'Growing up, I have seen a lot of kids struggle so it's easy for me to give back. I will always try to find different ways to give back to the kids and to Jamaica as a whole.'

Usain Bolt

Vital to the success of his Usain Bolt Foundation are board members (from left) Nugent Walker, Norman Peart and Zein Issa-Nakash.

Never forgetting his roots, Usain Bolt and Richard Byles of Sagicor Group Jamaica present a laptop to Dwayne Jarrett (centre), coach of William Knibb Memorial High School and Lorna Thorpe, head of the school's sports department.

Running for charity instead of gold.

Bolt's record-breaking feats over the 100m and 200m at the 2009 Berlin World Championships have been ranked by the IAAF as the #1 moments in its World Championships history.

Bolt: Jamaican Athletic Excellence and Resilience

Usain Bolt was on a roll. He seemed unstoppable, insuperable and indomitable. In 2003, he smashed the 200m and 400m high school championships records at the National Stadium, and then went on to shatter the World Junior record for the 200m at the CARIFTA Games in 2004; clocking 19.93 seconds, the fastest time in the world until the Olympics later that year.

He was expected to continue that dominance at the 2004 Athens Olympic Games. He did not. He crashed in the 200m heats due to injuries and returned to Jamaica amid a torrent of criticism and public disaffection. The press was brutal to him. He was still a fragile young man, sensitive to scorching criticism, and unaccustomed to it. That could have destroyed a lesser man.

But Usain St Leo Bolt is no mere mortal. His phoenix-like rise from the ashes of scorn and rejection to dizzying heights of Olympic glory four years later in Beijing is the stuff of which legends are made. It is precisely the stuff which created 'Legend' Bolt.

When coach Glen Mills found him, he was in the pit of dejection and self-pity. The inexorable march towards glory had been abruptly halted and he couldn't get his groove back. 'When he came to me, he had lost some of that spunk, some of his confidence because of what had happened to him,' Coach Mills said. 'You have to understand that at 15 he had taken the world by storm and then two years on, nothing was happening to him. The press and the public were disappointed and they gave him a hard time.' It was Coach Mills' task to pull out that spirit of resilience in him and to build back his confidence. Mills told him, 'I believe in you. You are the greatest sprinter God has ever made and if you believe in yourself as I believe in you, I can get you there no matter what happens and what is being said. The same people who are crucifying you will be the ones who will praise you when you win.'

The rest, as they say, is his history. It is a history which also mirrors Jamaica's – a history of struggle against the odds and against naysayers who have said this little country cannot fulfil its dream of independence. In its 55th year, Jamaica sees in Bolt its best: proud, purposeful, resilient, determined – a brand of excellence. Usain Bolt is a metaphor for Jamaica. His unconquerable, carefree yet focused spirit, his defiant optimism, his sense of style and deep immersion in the culture reflect the vibrancy and ethos of Jamaica. Usain's excellence incarnates Jamaica's excellence.

'We little but we tallawah' is a popular Jamaican saying, meaning the country punches above its weight in many areas. Sport represents a primary area in which we do so, and Usain Bolt is the iconic sporting hero. He embodies the values and attitudes so critical to national success: He possesses a rare combination of confidence and humility; respectfulness, optimism, team spirit, a passion for excellence – and discipline.

Here is a young man who never tires to point out how much he absolutely hates training. He is a party animal by instinct. He would rather get out of bed late, play his electronic games, have fun, chill out with friends and party all night. But as he has explained, he knows that to fulfil his potential he has to endure the pain of discipline. He has to train until it hurts – literally. His *I am Bolt* movie demonstrates that and shows the punishment which he puts his body through to attain excellence. It is not simply innate ability which keeps Usain at the top. It is gut-wrenching work.

Jamaicans are inspired and motivated by the feats of Usain Bolt. He might not have been officially designated a national hero, but to Jamaicans he undoubtedly is. They draw inspiration from a boy from a simple rural family who today rivals Bob Marley as the most famous Jamaican who has ever lived.

Usain Bolt knows how to come from behind, both literally and figuratively. He is the symbol of success for a small developing country like Jamaica, coming from behind economically, but seeing its collective dreams in 'The Legend'. Bolt is a metaphor of the excellence and resilience that characterise the Jamaican people. Another great Jamaican, reggae artiste Jimmy Cliff, put it this way in a famous song: *'You can get it if you really want, but you must try, try and try; try and try, you'll succeed at last.'*

Usain Bolt has blazed that path for Jamaica. In its 55th year, the country must follow in his footsteps.

Jamaica's Athletic Excellence. . .

Veronica Campbell-Brown – Three-time Olympic gold medallist

Asafa Powell – Former world's fastest man and sub 10-second king

Sherika Williams – Three-time Olympic silver medallist

Shelly-Ann Fraser-Pryce – Double Olympic Champion and joint national 100m record holder

Brigitte Foster-Hylton – Olympian and 2009
100m Hurdles World Champion

Melaine Walker – Former World Champion and
2008 Olympic 400m hurdles gold medallist
Kerron Stewart – Double Olympic silver medallist

Elaine Thompson – Double Olympic gold
medallist, joint national 100m record holder

Jermaine Gonzales – Olympian and 2011 IAAF
World Championships 4x400m relay bronze
medlalist

Britain's Prince Harry

*Sanya Richards-Ross
US Olympian*

**Yelena Isinbayeva
Russian World Record Pole Vaulter**

*Sebastian Coe
President, IAAF*

Michael Fennell
President, Jamaica Olympic
Association

Tyson Gay
US Olympic Sprinter

Allyson Felix
US Olympic
Sprinter

'I am inspired by him. To be able to carry on and do what he is doing is just unbelievable. You look up to someone like him.'

Mo Farah, British Olympic
Long Distance Runner

Liu Xiang
Chinese Olympic Hurdler

'Shaggy'
International Recording Artiste

'For me this is something big, it's something new and I'm thinking about my future on this one.'

Usain Bolt at the opening of his restaurant and sports lounge, Tracks and Records

Gary Matalon
CEO and Director, KLE Group

Denis O'Brien
Chairman of Digicel

'Usain Bolt has been pushing the limits...his whole career. We wanted to...find a way to thank Usain for everything he has done for his fans.'

Jonathan Adashek, Nissan's Chief Communications Officer

Lissant Mitchell
CEO, Scotia Investments
Jamaica

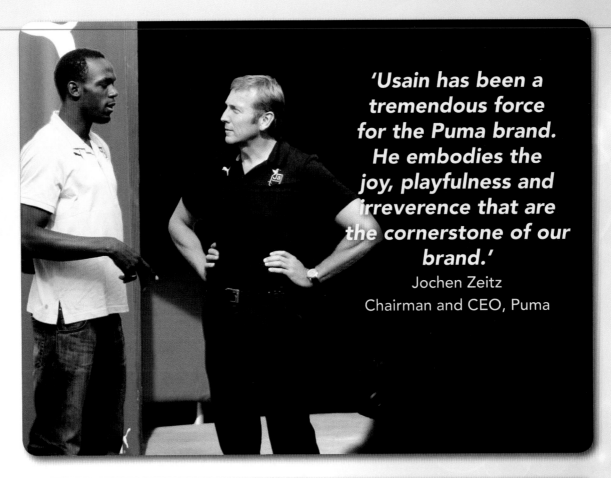

'Usain has been a tremendous force for the Puma brand. He embodies the joy, playfulness and irreverence that are the cornerstone of our brand.'

Jochen Zeitz
Chairman and CEO, Puma

Earl Jarrett
CEO, JN Group

Christopher Williams
Usain Bolt Foundation

Bolt hangs out with the I-Threes and
Minister Grange. From left: Judy Mowatt,
Marcia Griffiths, Minister Olivia 'Babsy'
Grange and Rita Marley

'Nitro Athletics is what track and field needs, a fresh way to present the sport.'
Usain Bolt

'No one has ever been part of something this much fun.'

declared Usain Bolt after leading the Bolt All-Stars team to victory in the inaugural Nitro Athletics in Melbourne, Australia, in February 2017

Usain Bolt:
The Long Goodbye

Goodbyes are often difficult. For track and field fans, witnessing Usain Bolt walk off into the sunset will be a lot worse.

If you experienced his golden reign, be grateful.

If you witnessed his transcending presence and gripping influence, consider it a blessing.

Hold on to it, because nothing lasts forever and there isn't much of a chance that the world will see another quite like him.

The iconic Jamaican sprinter is waving goodbye to the 'Office' after a *tour de force* that, in truth, saved a sport that was crying out for a crusader.

He will take with him a personality and charisma that transcended his unmatched on-track accomplishments and elevated him into pop culture itself as a synonym for speed.

When he walks away from track and field, he won't just leave with his spikes, but a little bit of magic will go with him.

Who would have thought that a lanky, thin-framed teenager from deep rural Jamaica, stumbling into track and field on the back of a pick-up game and the promise of a 'box lunch' to the winner, would become one of the most dominant and impactful athletes the sport had ever seen?

Bolt's absence from competition will no doubt have a far-reaching impact on the sport. The 'Bolt Effect' is real and has been at the forefront of track and field's relevance – a constant counter in the face of doping scandals, limited TV time and weak global marketability when compared to other key sports.

The brilliant Jamaican's ascension came at the right time for him and for the sport. Track and field needed a talisman, and with Bolt's refreshing personality and world-record runs in Beijing and Berlin gaining added legs because of the social-media surge, an icon was born, impossible became nothing.

Showing a healthy dose of 'cool' at the cameras before his races, beating his chest on the way to the finish line, DJ-ing after securing a gold medal, dancing for the world, dominating TV screens and advertising spots, enjoying massive endorsement deals – he is a magnet for media attention, and track and field has been better for it.

This type of enchantment is something that simply cannot be replaced.

That is something that the powers that be in the corridors of the IAAF recognise, with the Jamaican expected to carry his influence on the track with him in some sort of ambassadorial role once he unlaces his spikes for the final time.

That final time on the grand stage will take place at the World Championships in London.

Thirteen years after making his professional debut and 15 years after his first stride into international athletics recognition, Usain Bolt picked an old stamping ground as the site for his professional parting of the ways.

London is, of course, one of Jamaica and the Caribbean's largest outposts. Bolt's swansong will unfold in a city that is almost a second home for him.

The sprinter has spent most of his summer training camps in London with his Racers Track Club teammates over the years and is by now probably on a first-name basis with every nightclub owner and disc jock in the city.

In fact, Bolt has faced a starter in London on 15 occasions – almost half of those coming at the 2012 Olympic Games where he helped himself to three gold medals – like he did at the previous and subsequent instalments in Beijing and Rio de Janeiro, respectively.

The medals and records separate him from his peers, his personality and presence transcend the track, but while his accolades may gather dust one day, the true measure of the man and the athlete – his real legacy will be his impact on a crippled sport and the inspiration he will have on generations to come.

His ability to transcend race, age, class and every other dividing influence, as well as his story of motivation and encouragement – that in the face of challenges and unfavourable circumstances, teach that greatness can be achieved. This is his legacy: this is what he will leave with us when, for the final time, he crosses the line.

When his magical race ends, he would have inspired us all; he would have challenged us all; he would have made us all believe in the impossible.

As he prepares for another race – possibly marriage, fatherhood – life off the track in general; that's a script that is left to be written, a chapter left to be read.

In a year that will see his last, for the man of many firsts, this goodbye is difficult.

For track and field fans, Bolt's long farewell is an opportunity to appreciate a legend, to recognise the greatness of a man that took Jamaica and athletics –

'To di World'.

Bye 'VJ'

FINISH LINE

Wow!

It has been a magnificent journey that I could not have travelled without the support of my family, coaches, advisers and, friends and of course, my fans in Jamaica and all over the world.

It was not always easy. I had to work through and overcome injuries and many disappointments and setbacks throughout my career, but as I always say: 'Anything is possible, I don't think limits'.

That is the message I would like to leave with all young people who aspire to achieve greatness whether you are an athlete, an artiste or just a hard worker in your job or career, trying to make it in the world.

As I pass the baton and enter another phase of my career, I have every confidence in the ability of the upcoming generation of athletes, coaches and administrators to keep Jamaica's track and field at the pinnacle of world dominance. I will be there to help in any way I can and to cheer you on from the stands and the sidelines.

Thank you Jamaica; Thank you world for your support and for the energy that electrified me to become Lightning Bolt – Legend!

Usain Bolt

'Always, always gonna miss athletics, for sure.'
– Bolt speaking at Digicel Grand Prix at the National Stadium, Kingston, Jamaica Saturday, March 11, 2017